INSTITUTIONALISM

A STUDY OF THE ISSUES LEADING TO DIVISION AMONG CHURCHES OF CHRIST

A Study by Jeff Archer

2014 One Stone Press.
All rights reserved. No part of this book may be reproduced
in any form without written permission of the publisher.

Published by:
One Stone Press
979 Lovers Lane
Bowling Green, KY 42103

Printed in the United States of America

ISBN 10: 978-1941422-03-8
ISBN 13: 1-941422-03-9

Supplemental Materials Available:

➢ Answer Key

➢ Downloadable PDF

www.onestone.com

CONTENTS

Lesson 1	Authority - Overview	5
Lesson 2	Authority - The Conflict	9
Lesson 3	Authority - What Jesus Wants	13
Lesson 4	History	15
Lesson 5	Benevolent Institutions	23
Lesson 6	Benevolent Institutions (2)	27
Lesson 7	Sponsoring Church Arrangement	29
Lesson 8	Sponsoring Church Arrangement (2)	33
Lesson 9	Kitchens, Fellowship Halls, and Recreation	35
Lesson 10	Kitchens, Fellowship Halls, and Recreation (2)	39
Lesson 11	Denominationalism	41
Lesson 12	Denominationalism (2)	45

Lesson 1

AUTHORITY

Overview

The 1940's and 1950's were both wonderful and tragic for the church of the Lord. With WWII and the Great Depression moving into the past, a period of peace and prosperity set the stage for tremendous growth among churches of Christ. Unfortunately, with prosperity came innovations in how to spend the Lord's money and changes in the basic nature of the work of the church. The source of these changes did not spring so much from the teaching within local churches, but the lectureships of "brotherhood colleges", "brotherhood periodicals" and the pulpits of prominent preachers. These outside influences caused strife within local churches which led to division in city after city. Approximately 80-85% of congregations followed the more progressive, liberal, institutional belief while 15-20% remained with the conservative, anti, non-institutional belief. The effects of this division are still clear today. Very little contact is made between the two.

The purpose of this class is to examine, in an objective way, those issues dividing brethren in the 20th century and which continue to divide us now. Three reasons make this study important.

1. To be faithful to Jesus, the Head of His church, each individual and each local congregation must do what He wants. Examining the historical debate and division over these issues in light of Scripture will help us to understand Jesus' will more clearly.

2. Jesus wants all believers to be united. These issues still divide. The only way His goal will be accomplished is for all of us to mutually submit to His will. For this to happen, we must have open dialogue using an open Bible with those who differ from us. Studying these issues will prepare us for those discussions.

3. Those who do not learn from history are destined to repeat it.

6 INSTITUTIONALISM

We will be examining 5 topics in this set of lessons:

1) Authority
2) Benevolent institutions
3) Sponsoring church arrangement
4) Kitchens, fellowship halls and recreation
5) Denominationalism

Authority - the Basic Issue

The authority of the will of God must be recognized and submitted to by all disciples of Jesus Christ. If every disciple and every local church will do so—unity will prevail. When God reveals His will, there is only one correct position. While both positions in the debate over institutionalism acknowledge this fact, both cannot be right. Any teaching which is different from God's teaching must be abandoned. Mutually bowing in submission to the will of God is the only basis for unity.

1. Who has the authority to govern our lives (Matt. 28:18)? _____

2. What does it mean to be a disciple of Christ (Matt. 28:19-20)? _____
_____

3. Who is the head of the church and what does headship mean (Eph. 1:22-23; 5:23-24)? _____

4. What must we do to remain in fellowship with God (2 John 9-10)? _____
_____

   A. Where do we find this "doctrine?" _____

God's Pattern

5. When God instructed the children of Israel to build the tabernacle, how were they to build it (Exo. 25:8-9; Heb. 8:5)? _____
_____

   A. What does the word "pattern" mean? _____
_____

6. What was Paul's instruction to the evangelist Timothy (2 Tim. 1:13)? _____
_____

   A. Do these teachings change from generation to generation (2 Tim. 2:2)?
_____

   B. What was Paul's warning/prediction (2 Tim. 4 3-4)? _____
_____

   C. What was Timothy's responsibility (2 Tim. 4:1-2, 5)? _____
_____

AUTHORITY 7

7. Is there a particular way that Jesus wants His church to function (1 Tim. 3:14-15)? _____

   A. Skim through 1 Timothy and answer—What are some of the particular aspects of Jesus' pattern for His church? For example:—2:11-15—no women preachers. _____
   _____
   _____
   _____

   B. Skim through 1 Corinthians—What are some of the particular aspects of Jesus' pattern for His church? For example—2:1-5—preach only the message of Christ? _____
   _____
   _____
   _____

8. Does Jesus have a pattern for how He wants His church to function? ____
   _____

9. Can we understand the revelation of His pattern? _____

10. Are we following His pattern? _____

AUTHORITY (2)

The Conflict

When the issues were being debated in the 1940's, 50's and early 60's, most brethren agreed on how to determine what God wants us to do from Scripture.

On one occasion, brethren from the two opposing positions met in Arlington, TX in 1968 to discuss the issues. Although the two groups arrived at different conclusions, both acknowledged the same standard. In *The Arlington Meeting*, Roy Cogdill, representing the non-institutional position, stated, "But the question is raised, 'How may I know whether the New Testament teaches a thing or not?' This is not too difficult to answer. Brethren have always agreed, I think, that the Scriptures teach by three ways, though I have heard some expressions among Gospel preachers to the contrary in recent years: (1) by express command; (2) by approved example; (3) by necessary inference" (pp.32-33). J. D. Thomas, representing the institutional position, followed by saying, "I want you to know, and to hear me say it with my own words, that I believe the Bible is the only authority for us in religion. And the points that brother Cogdill made in this connection, I would agree wholeheartedly with" (p. 45).

Perhaps this is an oversimplification but the two basic differences between the two positions are:

1. The institutional position states the Scriptures are not specific in how the local church is to spend the Lord's money in benevolence or in cooperation. Each church is therefore at liberty to spend it with good judgment and to bind where God has not bound is without Biblical authority. The non-institutional position states the Scriptures are specific in many areas of how the local church is to spend the Lord's money in benevolence or in cooperation. Each church is therefore restricted and to go beyond is to act without Biblical authority.

2. The institutional position makes little or no distinction between what the individual Christian can do and what the local church can do. This leads to an institutionalizing of Christianity. The individual Christian is seen as accomplishing his work through

the institution/local church. The non-institutional position makes a clear distinction between what the individual Christian can do and what the local church can do. The Christian has certain responsibilities as an individual and certain responsibilities in joint participation with other Christians.

The position concerning authority among non-institutional brethren has remained relatively constant.

A wide spectrum of positions concerning authority exists among institutional brethren. Some have remained relatively constant with the early position while others have progressed into much looser positions. The "new hermeneutic" is an example. This "new" way of interpreting the Bible sees the words of Jesus as authoritative (relatively but not absolutely) and the words of the apostles as instructive, but not binding.

How To Determine What Jesus Wants Us To Do

■ Look in the Bible for statements or commands.

1. What were the apostles to teach the disciples of Christ (Matt. 28:19-20)? _____

2. How do we know how to remember Jesus' death (1 Cor. 11:23-25)? _____

3. What are we to do with members who "walk disorderly" (2 Thess. 3:6)? _____

4. What is the preacher to preach (2 Tim. 4:1-2)? _____

■ Look in the Bible for approved apostolic examples.

5. When are we to partake of the Lord's supper (Acts 20:7)? _____

6. What are we to do to be saved (Acts 2:38; 8:12-13; 9:18; 10:48 etc.)? _____

7. When are we to give and how much (1 Cor. 16:1-2)? _____

AUTHORITY (2)

■ **Look in the Bible for what is necessarily inferred.**

8. How often are we to partake of the Lord's supper (Acts 20:7)? _____

9. How did the Eunuch know about baptism (Acts 8:35-36)? _____

10. Is baptism immersion, sprinkling or pouring (Acts 8:38-39)? _____

11. Can the church rent, purchase or otherwise provide a place to worship (Heb.10:25)? _____

Cited

The Arlington Meeting. Marion, Ind.: Cogdill Foundation Publications, 1976. Print.

AUTHORITY (3)

Lesson 3

How to determine what Jesus wants—A Case Study

1. What was the question debated (Acts 15:1-2)? _____
_____

2. Why did Paul and Barnabas go to Jerusalem? Did they not already know the truth by revelation (Acts 15:1-2, 23-24)? _____
_____

3. To what did Peter, Paul and James appeal for authority?

   A. Acts 15:7 - _____

   B. Acts 15:8 - _____

   C. Acts 15:10-11 - _____

   D. Acts 15:12 - _____

   E. Acts 15:13-17 - _____

   F. Acts 15:19-20 - _____

4. To whom did they give credit for their answer (Acts 15:28)? _____

5. Was the outcome division or unity? Why? _____
_____

■ General and Specific Authority

6. The command for church discipline (2 Thess. 3:6,14).

14 INSTITUTIONALISM

- **Specific authority**

  A. Who is to be withdrawn from? _____

  B. What action is to be taken? _____

  C. What would be an unauthorized addition (what would violate the silence of the scriptures)? _____

- **General authority**

  A. How long does the process take from warning a brother to withdrawing from a brother? _____

  B. Should we write a letter, make a phone call or have a personal visit in the discipline process? _____

  C. What would be an unauthorized addition (what would violate the silence of the scriptures)? _____
  _____

7. The command to sing (Eph.5:19).

- **Specific authority**

  A. What are we to sing? _____
  _____

  B. What kind of music are we to use? _____
  _____

  C. What would be an unauthorized addition (what would violate the silence of the scriptures)? _____
  _____

- **General authority**

  A. Where are we to sing? _____

  B. Can we use song books, sing from memory, project songs on a screen? _____
  _____

  C. What would be an unauthorized addition (what would violate the silence of the scriptures)? _____
  _____

Lesson 4

HISTORY

In this lesson, we will examine the history of the conflict from both sides. Please read the two following accounts from opposing viewpoints and be prepared to discuss your impressions in class.

Bill Hall, who stands opposed to institutionalism, has delivered 3 lessons in recent years describing the issues causing the division: Church-Supported Orphan's Homes, The Sponsoring Church Arrangement and Kitchens and Fellowship Halls. Below is a portion of the first lesson. To view the full transcript go to: *http://www.cvillechurch.com/RestudyingTheIssuesOfThe50sAnd60s.htm.*

To hear the sermons preached go to: *http://www.westendchurch.com/online_sermons.htm.*

CHURCH-SUPPORTED ORPHAN'S HOMES: WHAT WAS THE ISSUE?

It was a difficult time. I don't know that I could in any way picture for you, if you didn't live then, just how difficult that time was. Back somewhere in the mid-50s, in the pages of the Gospel Advocate, a quarantine was called for against all those who preached the gospel who opposed any institutional setup. That was about the time I started preaching. Meetings were canceled, churches were divided, preachers were fired. I see one of Irven Lee's daughters back in the audience; Brother Lee was one of them who was fired. He was one of the best men I ever knew. Families were divided in sentiment. It was such a difficult time. Oftentimes when we go through issues like that, people are not listening to one another. We're so anxious to know what we're going to say next, or how we're going to answer the person, that we really don't listen. And I really think that what happened when we went through those difficult times was that many people had no idea what the issue was. And so, what I hope to do today, and next Sunday and the following Sunday, is clarify what the issues were. What were some of the arguments back and forth? My purpose is to help us to look back and say, "Is that really what happened?" I'm going to be as fair as I can be in regard to just exactly what happened.

Now this afternoon, we'll talk about the orphan's homes. What was the issue in regard to the orphan's home? I think it just blows a lot of people's minds to even think that any church of Christ would have thought that you ought not to support an orphan's home. What is the issue?

What Was Not The Issue?

Well, let's talk about what the issue is not. The issue is not whether or not orphans should be cared for. That's easily answered. James 1:27: "Pure and undefiled religion before God and the Father is this: to visit orphans and widows in their affliction, and to keep oneself unspotted from the world." Orphans and widows are to be cared for. That was never one of the issues.

A second thing that was not the issue was whether or not the church ought to take care of orphans. That may surprise some of you, but when these problems first began, very few people ever even questioned whether the church should take care of orphans. That question didn't even arise until quite some time after these things began to be discussed. When these issues first developed and people began to voice objection to the orphan's home, nearly every church thought that it would be all right to support and take care of orphans even from the church treasury. I think that's surprising to a lot of people. Now the issue shifted and we're going to see that this became an issue. But that was not where the issue really lay.

The third thing I think we need to say, and I believe everybody knows this, that this was not a question of who was loving and caring and who wanted to help orphans the most. That's not what it was. Now in the heat of the time there were those who looked at some of us and said, "These people are just uncaring people. They just don't believe in caring for orphans." Well, of course that wasn't true and history has shown that we who objected to orphan's homes supported by churches were just as caring and loving and wanting to help as those who stood in favor of the institution. That's just not where the issue lay.

What Was The Issue?

Well, somebody asks, just what then was the issue? Well, the issue involved what I'm going to call "A Middleman Organization" standing between the church and the work to be done. You know in business, sometimes we talk about eliminating the middleman. What do we mean by that? Well, by the time a product leaves the factory, you've got to pay the delivery man, you've got to pay the wholesaler, you've got to pay the retailer, and by the time all of them get their money, you have paid too much; so go to the factory, and eliminate the middleman. It doesn't matter about business. But basically, what God did: He did not arrange for any middleman, any middleman organizations.

The issue was basically this: You have the local churches - if I may picture them as being circles here - and then you had a board of directors. We'll just call it an institutional board.

Now, this institutional board is made up of Christians from many different churches. You might have two or three from Birmingham, you might have one or two from Jasper, you might have one or two from Athens. All of these come together as a board. And the money goes from the churches to the institutional board which in turn, then, provides housing, supervision, food, and whatever is needful for the care of these orphans. There's the issue: this institutional board that provides oversight for the work of churches of Christ.

Now somebody will say, "What is wrong with that?" The answer is: There is no authority for this institutional board as an overseeing body for the work of churches. And those of us who objected just raised the question, "Where is the authority for this board that stands between the churches and the work that needs to be done?"

Several passages come to mind when we talk about the necessity of authority. Colossians 3:17: "And whatever you do in word or deed, do all in the name of the Lord Jesus, giving thanks to God the Father through Him." Now, if this has the authority of Jesus Christ behind it, then we can do it in His name. But if Jesus has never authorized this, then we cannot do this in the name of Jesus. We can say we're doing it in the name of Jesus, but the only thing we can actually do in the name of Jesus is that which He has authorized. You cannot do anything in anybody's name unless that person has authorized that which is to be done. Another passage that was pointed out was 2 Timothy 3:16-17: "All Scripture is given by inspiration of God, and is profitable for doctrine, for reproof, for correction, for instruction in righteousness, that the man of God may be complete, thoroughly equipped for every good work." Consequently, if this is a good work - to have this board of directors providing oversight for the churches - then you're going to find that it's in the Scriptures. That's what we pointed out. Another passage oftentimes used was 2 John, verse 9: "Whoever transgresses and does not abide in the doctrine of Christ does not have God. He who abides in the doctrine of Christ has both the Father and the Son."

So the question we raised was: Is this institutional board in the doctrine of Christ, or is this outside the doctrine of Christ? If it's in the doctrine of Christ, we need it. If it's outside the doctrine of Christ, then we cannot have anything to do with it. So the obligation falls on the shoulders of brethren who support this to show the scriptural authority by which this could be done. . . .

The Shift In Issue

Now, in time there came a shift in issue. I do not know exactly when this took place. But somewhere down the way, somebody raised the question: Does the church really have the responsibility to take care of orphans in the first place?

Doesn't the Bible talk about the church helping needy saints? Now, that was an issue that arose after the institutional issue had been fought for quite some time.

Now, in answer to that, let's get our Bibles and turn to Acts 2:44 ... Acts 4:34 ... Acts 11:29 ... Rom. 15:25-26 ... I Cor. 16:1-2 ... 2 Cor. 8 and 9 ... And we could just keep on going: it's the saints, it's the brethren, it's any among them. Those are expressions used. . . .

And in some ways, this shift of issue was unfortunate. In other ways, it was fortunate. It was unfortunate in that it took the focus of the people away from the institutional issue and put it on something else. And as you would imagine, from that point on, most of those who were going to debate this question wanted to debate the limited benevolence issue instead of the institutional issue. So all of a sudden there was a shift. We'd had discussion after discussion after discussion over this institutional board, but all of a sudden there's a shift, and most of the discussion then focused on whether the church could help orphan children.

But that was a shift in emphasis that a lot of people in this generation do not realize took place. And of course that was a more emotional issue. This shift of issue took the eyes of the people away from the institutional board, an unscriptural organization, and caused them to focus on whom the church should help from its treasury. This left the churches vulnerable to similar institutional arrangements that might arise in the future.

Now, it's fortunate that it happened in that it forced many of us who never had done it before to say: just whom does the church have a responsibility to help?

And I'm glad that I was forced to do that. It forced me to go through the Scriptures, just as I have just now gone through the Scriptures, and to say, "Just who is to be helped by the church?" Anytime we're forced to look into the Scriptures regarding any question, that of course is good. But the issue changed. A lot of people never understood that shift of issues. . . .

Somebody says, "But this is really more of a historical thing; we don't hear about orphan's homes anymore." I would suspect if I were to ask for a show of hands: how many people have heard anything very much about the church support of orphan's homes in the last ten years, there would be very few hands go up.

There are still some churches that do it, but someone might be asking, "why worry about all this?" While the orphan home issue is almost a past issue now, there are other institutions asking churches for help that function under an institutional board. This is true, for instance, of David Lipscomb University, Freed Hardeman, Mars Hill over in Florence, or other schools that we could name. Batsell Barrett Baxter, before his death, wrote a tract called "Questions and Issues of the Day", and here's what he wrote: "Some who will agree that the church can contribute to an orphan's home are not convinced that the church can contribute to a Christian school. It is difficult to see a significant difference. As far as principle is concerned, the orphan's home and the Christian school must stand or fall together." This tract argues for the church support of schools, based upon acceptance of church support of orphan homes.

If we lose sight of the institutional issue, and begin to see the whole orphan's home question as a question of whether the church should help orphans or not, then we leave ourselves so vulnerable to this kind of thing happening again. In the mid-1800s, it was a missionary society. How is a missionary society set up? It is with an institutional board providing oversight for the work of churches of Christ. Then we come to the mid-1900s and we go through a battle again and how were the orphan's homes set up? Exactly the same way. And then there's the battle about whether the church can support schools or not. How are the schools set up? In exactly the same way. If we don't keep our attention focused on the institutional board as the primary issue, it leaves us vulnerable to similar institutions that are going to arise. What will be the institution of the mid-2000s? I don't know! But let us understand that there is no authority for churches of Christ to do their work under the oversight of an institutional board. Churches of Christ do their work under the oversight of the elders of each local church.

So let's go back. Is the question of whom the church should support an important question? Yes, that's an important question. Any Bible question is an important question. But let's not allow that question to turn our attention away from this issue of an institutional board standing between churches and the work to be done...

■·■·■·■·■·■

The following lesson was delivered at the 2006 Spring Church of Christ Lectureship, Spring, TX. Its author, Dub McClish, is a preacher who supports institutionalism. In his lesson he discussed the issues of: "Anti-located Preacher", "Anti-Variety-of-Order-of-Worship", "Anti-Bible College", "Anti-Sunday School", "Anti-Literature", "Anti-Baptistery", "anti-multiple cup" before coming to the portion from which we quote. For the complete lesson see *http://www.scripturecache.com/resources/HISTORY+OF+ANTI-ISM.pdf.*

A HISTORY OF "ANTI-ISM" FROM THE 19TH CENTURY TO THE PRESENT BY DUB MCCLISH

The Second Half of the Century

By the middle point of the century, most of the "anti" hobbies previously reviewed had been exposed and largely defeated except for small, random pockets of influence. The vast majority of the church was marching onward and was poised to enter an unprecedented (at least in modern times) period of numerical growth. However, as the familiar platitude states, "The devil never sleeps." The most devastating of all "anti" doctrines and offensives would soon be thrust upon an unsuspecting brotherhood.

The "Anti-Cooperation" and "Anti-Orphan-Home" Issues

Since the apostolic era, congregations had worked together to preach the Gospel and help the helpless. However, a few brethren concluded that such cooperation was unauthorized. Likewise, for several generations, congregations had (with little objection, except an occasional extremist such as Sommer and his followers) established and/or supported out of their treasuries homes to supply the needs of otherwise homeless children. The brethren who advocated the new doctrine that opposed congregational cooperation also asserted that congregations were unauthorized to support such homes in this manner (thus reviving this aspect of Sommerism).

The prime movers in this campaign had formerly participated without qualms, much less opposition, in both of these arrangements, which they suddenly began to proscribe. Foy E. Wallace, Jr., commenting on the major tenets of the mid-century "antis," made this very point:

> Every one of these points that have been made an issue were previously preached and practiced by the leaders of the new party themselves and only lately have been seized in the frustration of grasping for issues where there were no issues, to form their party line.[25]

These newly-enlightened brethren decided they must bind their scruples upon the entire church. Their fierce and determined campaign against what they variously call "institutionalism," "liberalism," and "digression" has likely wrought more rack and ruin in the church than did all of the previous "anti" issues combined.

The "anti-cooperation" campaign's beginning date is usually marked in 1950. Actually, Roy E. Cogdill, one of the leaders of the faction, fired the initial salvos somewhat earlier. On August 9, 1946, Cogdill, who lived in Houston, Texas, at the time, delivered a lecture on "Inter-Congregational Cooperation" in the East Oakland, California, church building. More than four hundred assembled brethren since heard him advance the doctrine "that no two congregations could scripturally cooperate in anything without violating each other's local autonomy."[26] Ira Y. Rice, Jr., and Robert R. Price heard Cogdill deliver the sermon and tried to warn brethren of his doctrine, but brethren apparently thought the doctrine was so palpably ridiculous that, even if someone taught such, no one would believe it.

When the campaign's leaders got underway in earnest, they specifically targeted the Herald of Truth radio program, which was sponsored by the Highland Church in Abilene, Texas, and was overseen by its elders. This program was being aired on several radio stations, and other congregations were sending financial support to Highland to enable it to continue and to increase its coverage. With a four-year head start on the "anticooperation" theme, the April 20, 1950, issue of Gospel Guardian began open warfare against what it labeled "apostasy" and a "new digression."

... In its first anniversary issue (May 4, 1950), it carried the following editorial statement relating to its dearest dogmas and its editorial aim: We are committed to battle and that without restraint, yes even to the point of division on exactly the same basis that those who opposed the instrumental music divided the church seventy-five years ago. This warning from Cogdill and Tant leading could only be understood as a declaration of war. Thereafter these two men dedicated The Gospel Guardian (indeed, their lives) to opposing cooperation and children's homes. Through its pages, through preaching, and through publication of tracts they spread their hobbies widely.

As they began to gain influence among some preachers and as these preachers began to disturb, divide, and/or steal congregations, faithful brethren realized that they must respond to and refute these doctrines with the Truth. . . .

Analogous "Anti" Issues

Predictably, the two foregoing "anti" contentions spawned additional "anti" hobbies (although not all who rode off on the "anti-cooperation" and "anti-orphan home" horses rode off on all of the sub-hobbies). These kindred doctrines included (1) declaring it sinful to eat a physical meal on church property and (2) declaring it sinful for the church to help render physical aid to anyone who is not a Christian (i.e., the "saints only" doctrine).

The anti-Bible class, anti-literature, anti-women-teacher, anti-located- preacher, antivariety- of-worship-order, anti-multiple-cups, and anti-Bible-college positions were generally recognized as extreme by most brethren through the efforts of stalwart men who exposed their fallacies. They therefore captured only a relatively small percentage of congregations and had largely run their course by the1940s.

Although, as earlier noted, all of the "anti" doctrines make the same basic arguments and the same basic mistakes in Biblical interpretation, for some reason(s) the more recent "anti" doctrines attracted far more adherents than previous ones had done.

Many preachers succumbed to them and aligned themselves with them, and at least a few hundred congregations were captured by them. Florida Christian College in Tampa, Florida came under the influence of this faction and it continues in this alignment as Florida College. One writer estimates that, before resistance and refutation slowed their efforts, they had captured perhaps ten percent of the brotherhood.[29] While these "anti" brethren continue to propagate their doctrine, refusing to fellowship those who will not bow to their personal scruples, they have not made any major gains in the past four decades. . . .

Conclusion

May we all earnestly strive ever to discern just the things God has authorized his people to do, both for His congregations and His individual saints, and then may we earnestly do those very things and those alone. May we also all allow the lessons of history to prevent those who would bind upon us their own rules, laws, doctrines, restrictions, regulations, personal scruples, and other optional matters as if they were the law of God. Such is the essence of "anti-ism," in whatever symptom it may manifest itself.

Please record your observations below:

From Bill Hall's lesson

_____
_____
_____
_____
_____
_____
_____

From Dub McClish's lesson

_____
_____
_____
_____
_____
_____
_____

BENEVOLENT INSTITUTIONS

During the late 1800's, a heightened social conscience was developing in the US. Abraham Lincoln signed the Emancipation Proclamation in 1863 which lead to a social movement for racial equality. Susan B. Anthony and others pushed for a woman's right to vote beginning a social movement for women's rights. Many workers were being exploited, so labor unions sprang up. Individual solutions were not emphasized. It was a time for establishing institutions to solve the problems. Orphans were sent to orphanages, the mentally ill to mental institutions and the hungry to soup kitchens. At the same time, many "theologians", perhaps swayed by the quickly rising popularity of Charles Darwin's *Origin of the Species* among the "educated circles," turned their attention away from saving the soul from Hell to saving the downtrodden from their difficult life on this earth. Denominational Churches began forming institutions to care for the world's needy.

Brethren are usually the last to jump on the bandwagon, but slowly they were influenced. In the early 1900s, brethren organized orphanages. Christians from several churches formed a governing body and solicited funds from a number of churches to care for the orphans.

Most if not all of the orphanages in the US have closed their doors switching to the foster care system. People realized children did not need to be institutionalized, but put in a home. In time, the same has happened to many of the orphan's homes run by brethren, but the principle of church supported benevolent institutions is still alive and well. Since then, many other institutions have been established by churches of Christ: nursing homes, day care centers, K-12 schools and colleges, Bible colleges, the "Church of Christ Disaster Relief Effort" and others.

In the next lesson we will examine whether the church is authorized to build and maintain a benevolent institution. In this lesson we will examine—who is the church to help from its treasury? Can a church help non-Christians as well as Christians from the church's treasury? Is there a difference in what the church can do and what the individual can do? To answer each of these questions we will examine command, apostolic example and/or necessary inference.

24 INSTITUTIONALISM

In each of the following contexts please look for: Who helped the needy? Who was helped? Why were they in need? Was the help short or long term?

Local Church Action

1. Acts 2:44-45 - _____

2. Acts 4:34-37 - _____

3. Acts 6:1-6 - _____

4. Acts 11:27-30 - _____

5. Rom. 15:25-27 - _____

6. 1 Cor. 16:1-4 - _____

7. 2 Cor. 8:1-4 - _____

8. 1 Tim. 5:3-16 - _____

9. Based on the scriptures just studied, please fill out the following chart.

SCRIPTURE	Who Is Helped?		Who Helped Them?	
	Christians	Non-Christians	Local Church	Benevolent Institution
Acts 2:44-45				
Acts 4:32-35				
Acts 6:1-6				
Acts 11:27-30				
Rom. 15:22-29				
1 Cor. 16:1-4				
2 Cor. 8, 9				
1 Tim. 3:5-16				

Individual Action

10. 1 Tim. 5:3-16 - _____

11. Gal. 6:10 - _____

12. James 1:27 - _____

Lesson 6

BENEVOLENT INSTITUTIONS (2)

The question is not whether individual Christians can band together to build and maintain a benevolent institution. Many very good organizations have been established to help the needy. The question is whether there is scriptural authority for a church to build and maintain a benevolent institution.

Please keep the verses from the following lesson in mind as you answer the following questions. In answering each question, please cite the verse(s) which would authorize such a practice. Please note: Some of the answers may not have any verses to support the action—it is therefore NOT authorized.

1. If a member of the local church is hurt and unable to work, is there authority for the local church to help him/her financially? _____ verse(s) _____

    A. Is there authority for a church to establish and maintain an employment office? _____ verse(s) _____

2. If a member of the local church has some accident or physical problem but is unable to pay for necessary medical help, is there authority for the local church to help him financially? _____ verse(s) _____

    A. Is there authority for a local church to establish and maintain a hospital, an assisted living home or a nursing home? _____ verse(s) _____

3. If a member of the local church wants to go to college but cannot afford it, is the local church authorized to pay his college tuition? _____ verse(s) _____

    A. Is there authority for the local church to build and maintain a college? _____ verse(s) _____

4. If the church receives a phone call from a woman who is not a member of the church needing help with her rent or utilities, can the local church help her financially? _____ verse(s) _____

INSTITUTIONALISM

   A. Is there authority for a local church to establish and maintain an apartment complex for the needy? _____ verse(s) _____

5. A widow who is a member can no longer care for herself. Is the local church authorized to help her financially? _____ verse(s) _____

   A. Who has the first responsibility? _____ verse(s) _____

   B. Can she be helped long term? _____ verse(s) _____

6. A hurricane/flood/drought/war destroys an area of the world. Many Christians and non-Christians are affected. Is there authority for the local church to help financially Christians who are in need? _____ verse(s) _____

   A. Who has the first responsibility: the local church where he/she is a member or other churches? _____ verse(s) _____

   B. Can a church from, for example, Alabama, take from its treasury and send financial help to Christians in the church in Georgia who are in need? _____ verse(s) _____

   To whom do they send the aid? _____

   C. Can individual Christians send financial help to Christians and non-Christians? _____ verse(s) _____

   D. Can Christians start a "Church of Christ relief agency" and ask for funds from churches and individuals to help Christians and non-Christians? _____ verse(s) _____

7. A group of Christians decide to help orphans by building and maintaining an orphan's home. Can they ask other Christians and non-Christians to fund their Home? _____ verse(s) _____

   A. Can they solicit funds from local churches and is it authorized for those churches to contribute? _____ verse(s) _____

SPONSORING CHURCH ARRANGEMENT

Lesson 7

The organization of the Lord's church is simple, efficient and effective. The church universal is made up of Christians who listen to the Head of the church, Jesus Christ. He has given instructions in His word and as Christians follow His word, they are submitting to His leadership. While much of the Lord's work is to be accomplished by individual Christians, some of His work is to be done by the local church. A local church is a group of Christians who have banded together to work as one. Each local church is to be organized with a set of elders as its leaders, deacons as 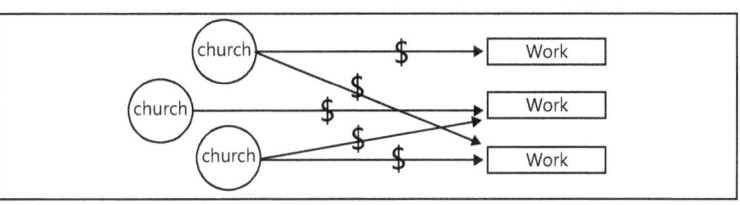 special servants, preachers as proclaimers of the gospel and members fulfilling other important roles. God's pattern for the church is sufficient to carry out its vital work. Members give money to the local church. The elders oversee the pool of money and, with it, accomplish the Lord's work.

One of the first widespread departures from the New Testament pattern came in the area of church organization. From the simple structure of elders leading each church came a developing hierarchy which led to the immense organization of the Roman Catholic Church. Members gave money to the local church which in turn sent the money to Rome where it was decided how the money was to be spent. The Roman Church then sent the money to benevolent and evangelistic institutions it had established to carry out the work of the Church.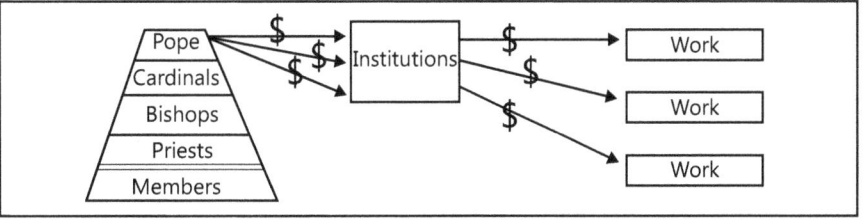

INSTITUTIONALISM

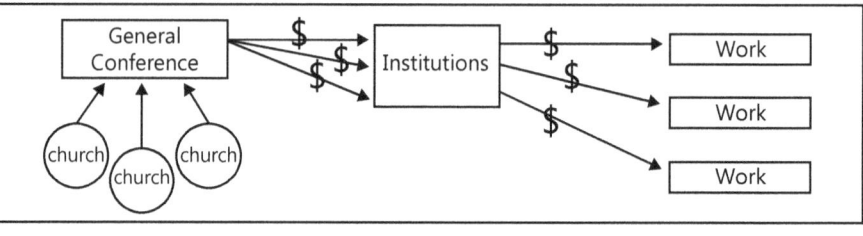

Reformation sought to reform many of the errors of Catholicism but, unfortunately, many of its departures were retained. Synods, conferences, societies, and boards were organized to govern newly formed denominations. Members gave money to the local churches which sent the money to the headquarters of the denomination which determined how the money was to be spent. The headquarter sent the money to institutions established to do the work of the denomination.

The Restoration Movement saw tremendous growth as people came out of denominationalism to return to the simple pattern of the gospel of Christ. It was not long, however, before men wanted to organize beyond the teaching of the Bible. The American Christian Missionary Society was started by men like Alexander Campbell who believed such an institution was necessary for the church to carry out its work in evangelism. Members gave money to the local church. The church sent the money to the missionary society which decided which preachers were to be supported and where they would go. The majority of churches supported the Missionary Society and instrumental music and were called Disciples of Christ and/or the Christian Churches. A minority of churches opposed such innovations. Most were called churches of Christ.

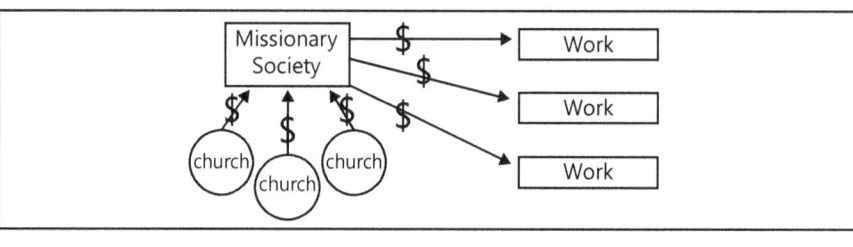

Among churches of Christ after World War II, evangelistic awareness was high and motivation was strong to evangelize areas of the world recently torn by war. A new form of organization emerged—the Sponsoring Church Arrangement. The elders of the Sponsoring Church took on a work which was too large to be sustained financially by the local church where they were elders. They solicited funds from the treasuries of any and all other local churches. When they received these contributions, they then oversaw the distribution of the money and, many times, the newly formed local churches. Members gave money to the local church. Local churches sent money to the elders of one Sponsoring Church which took on the oversight of the evangelistic work in a particular country. For example, the Broadway church of Christ in Lubbock, Texas designated itself as the sponsoring church to evangelize Germany. The Union Avenue church of Christ in Memphis, Tennessee, became the sponsoring church to evangelize Japan. The Highland church of Christ in Abilene, Texas became the sponsoring church of a nation wide radio program called the Herald of Truth.

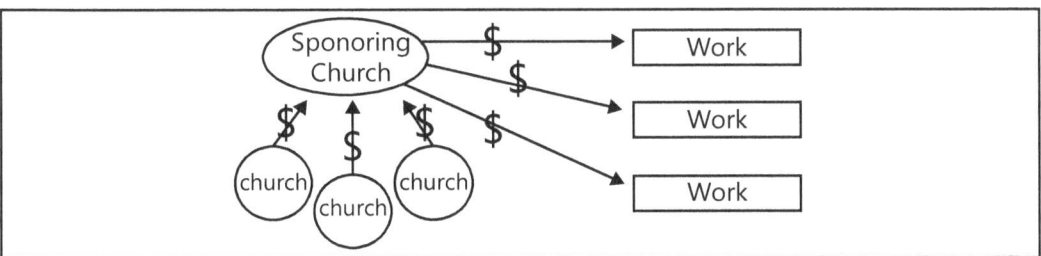

In its inception this Sponsoring Church arrangement was perhaps a response to the criticism of the board of directors overseeing the benevolent institutions. (See chart above). These Sponsoring Churches claimed their work was overseen by a set of elders. In a short time, however, these Sponsoring Churches built institutions with boards of directors to accomplish the work. The departure from the scriptural pattern was compounded.

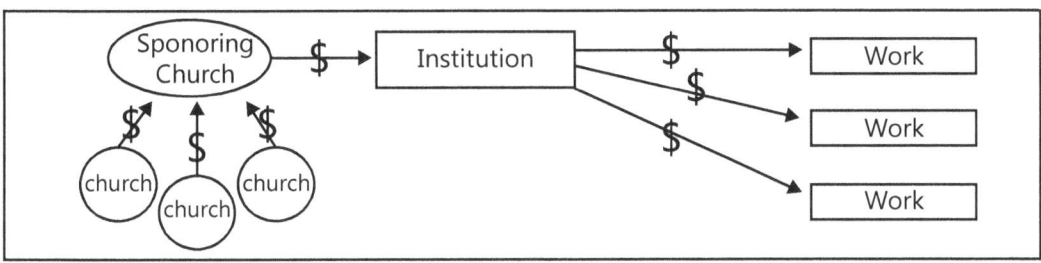

Today, this same organizational structure is used in a variety of ways. (See chart above). "In Russia, out of 23 congregations established through the SCU mission program, 19 of them have eldership oversight from America," (Sewell Hall's article on "*Institutionalism,*" Christianity Magazine, Feb. 1996) In Honduras, the Westover Hills church of Christ in Austin, Texas works as the sponsoring church through the Baxter Institute in the capital, Tegucigalpa. It holds the deed to many of the church buildings and oversees who preaches in local churches under its control. Calls for even more dramatic departures are being made by men like Bob Douglas, a member of the church of Christ, speaking at the Central church of Christ in Irving, Texas, "We must give up our present focus on a perfect New Testament pattern... We must foster more extra-congregational organizations, such as regional fellowships of informal associations which bring together the resources of many congregations and in turn cooperate with other churches, other denominations, in meeting the world's needs."

The question with each of these organizational structures is, what does God authorize?

Local Church Organization

1. How did the apostle Paul, through the direction of the Holy Spirit, organize churches (Acts 14:21-23)? _____

2. Why did Paul leave Titus in Crete (Titus 1:5)? _____

3. How was the church at Philippi organized (Phil. 1:1)? _____

4. What is the work of the eldership (Acts 20:28)? _____

Extent of the Oversight of the Elders

5. For what are the elders responsible (Acts 20:28)? _____

6. For what are the elders responsible (1 Peter 5:1-4)? _____

7. Is there any authority for one eldership having oversight of the work of another church? _____

SPONSORING CHURCH ARANGEMENT (2)

Lesson 8

Sometimes Christians who oppose the Sponsoring Church Arrangement are called "anti-cooperation." The fact is, the Bible teaches local churches can cooperate. The question is—how? There is a difference between **collective** and **concurrent cooperation**. To illustrate, several homes are in a subdivision. The subdivision needs to be cleaned up. **"Collective cooperation"** could be carried out by each homeowner giving money to an Homeowners Association (HOA) which in turn hires Bubba's Handyman Service to do the work. Perhaps, in the subdivision lives widow Smith who is unable to contribute. Each homeowner could contribute a little more to the HOA for Bubba to clean up her yard also. **"Concurrent cooperation"** could be carried out by each homeowner making his own arrangements for the clean up of his own yard. He might do the job himself or hire Bubba to do it for him. Widow Smith would be taken care of by each neighbor helping to clean her yard or each sending a check to Bubba to take care of it.

Concurrent cooperation among churches is taught in scripture. The scriptures are silent about collective cooperation.

Cooperation in Evangelism

1. When the church in Jerusalem heard of the conversions in Antioch, what did it do (Acts 11:22)? _____

    A. Did the church in Jerusalem become the sponsoring church of the church in Antioch? _____ verse(s) _____

    B. When Barnabas sent for Saul, did he get permission from the sponsoring church in Jerusalem? _____ verse(s) _____

2. When Saul and Barnabas went to preach the gospel, who sent them out (Acts 13:1-3)? _____

34 INSTITUTIONALISM

3. When Paul and Barnabas returned from their trip, what did they do (Acts 14:26-28)?
_____

4. At the end of their trip, what did Paul and Barnabas do (Acts 14:21-23)? _____
_____

   A. Was the church in Antioch the sponsoring church of the ministry of Paul and Barnabas? _____ verse(s) _____

   B. Did the church of Antioch take the oversight of these newly formed churches? _____ verse(s) _____

5. Who has the primary responsibility to pay the preacher (1 Cor. 9:11-14)? _____
_____

6. What had the church in Philippi done for Paul? Phil. 4:15-18 (Acts 17:1-9) _____
_____

A. Was this money sent through a sponsoring church or directly to Paul? _____
_____

B. Was the church in Philippi Paul's sponsoring church? _____
verse(s) _____

7. When Paul was in Corinth, he received money from other churches (2 Cor. 11:7-9, Acts 18:1-18).

   A. Was the money sent to the church in Corinth or directly to Paul? _____

   B. Did the money come from a sponsoring church or from several churches each sending their part? _____

Cooperation in Benevolence

8. When the church in Antioch sent money to the needy brethren in Judea, how did it do so (Acts 11:27-30)? _____

A. Did the church in Antioch become the sponsoring church of the needy in Judea? Did they send money to a sponsoring church? _____ verse(s) _____

9. When the church in Corinth, along with other churches from Galatia, sent money for the needy saints, how did it do so (1 Cor. 16:1-4)? _____
_____

A. Why did the church need to choose a messenger to carry the gift (1 Cor. 16:3)? __
_____

10. What is the responsibility of a church when there are needy saints in other churches (2 Cor. 8:12-15)? _____
_____

Lesson 9

KITCHENS, FELLOWSHIP HALLS AND RECREATION

Toward the end of the 1800's, the religious world was greatly influenced by two major false teachings. Among the intellectuals, Evolution was quickly replacing belief in God as the Creator. In addition, liberal critics were undercutting belief that the Bible was inspired of God. Because of these two influences, many denominations changed their focus from the salvation from sin to salvation from economic and social injustice. Denominations involved themselves in building and maintaining institutions for the betterment of man on the earth (orphans homes, hospitals, schools, soup kitchens, etc.). In time the focus of the work of these churches become much more superficial to include social activities for the members (especially young people) and a focus on entertainment rather than worship in their services.

From the early 1900s among churches of Christ, it was not uncommon to have "dinner on the grounds" during gospel meetings or occasionally after worship services. Christians brought food and shared in a "pot luck" style meal under a shade tree on the church's property. In 1947, M. Norvel Young, while speaking during the lectureship at Abilene Christian University, encouraged churches to build new buildings to include cooking facilities and a large room for social events. This idea did not catch on right away by the majority of churches. Those who followed this advice defensively said, "We're going to have Bible classes in this room too." In the latter part of the 60s and into the 70s, many churches began building additional buildings to accommodate social functions, following the tend in the denominational world. Social activity became part of the work of the church along side evangelism, edification and benevolence. The emphasis on social activities was defended as necessary to keep the young people faithful to the Lord. Some churches hired "youth ministers" who, many times, were essentially social directors for the youth. Additional paid ministers were hired to organize other social activities. Basketball, softball and other sports teams were formed which competed in leagues against teams from the denominational world.

The question is not whether it is good for Christians to socialize together. The question is whether it is part of the work of the church. The vast majority of churches who believed in church supported benevolent institutions and the sponsoring church arrangement, also added social activities to their work. The vast majority of churches who opposed church supported benevolent institutions and the sponsoring church arrangement also opposed social activities as part of the work of the church.

"Fellowship"

Many times those who built "fellowship halls" justified themselves by saying that God wanted them to have fellowship. Therefore, they built fellowship halls in which they eat, drink, and play. However, the Bible never uses the word "fellowship" in this sense.

The word "fellowship" (koinonia) means "(a) communion, fellowship, sharing in common . . . (b) that which is the outcome of fellowship, a contribution" (Vines Dictionary). The idea is when two or more people jointly participate/share in an activity, they are in fellowship. Although the word "fellowship" could mean sharing in any activity, the Bible **always** uses "fellowship" to refer to sharing in spiritual activities, never social activities. While it is true the disciples of Christ shared in meals together in their homes (Lk.5:29; 10:40-42; Acts 2:46), it was never called "fellowship".

Listed below are all the occurrences of the word (koinonia) translated: "fellowship," "communion," "contribution," and "sharing" in the New Testament. Please read through them and observe how the word is used.

- Act 2:42 - "fellowship"
- Rom. 15:26 - "contribution for the poor among the saints"
- 1 Cor. 1:9 - "the fellowship of His Son"
- 1 Cor. 10:16 - "the communion of the blood of Christ . . . the communion of the body of Christ"
- 2 Cor. 6:14 - "what communion has light with darkness"
- 2 Cor. 8:4 - "the fellowship of the ministering to the saints"
- 2 Cor. 9:13 - "sharing with them"
- 2 Cor. 13:14 - "the communion of the Holy Spirit"
- Gal. 2:9 - "the right hand of fellowship"
- Eph. 3:9 - "the fellowship of the mystery"
- Phil. 1:5 - "fellowship in the gospel"
- Phil. 2:1 - "fellowship of the Spirit"
- Phil. 3:10 - "the fellowship of His sufferings"
- Phile. 6 - "the sharing of your faith"
- Heb. 13:16 - "to share"
- 1 John 1:3 - "fellowship with us . . . fellowship is with the Father"
- 1 John 1:6 - "we have fellowship with Him"
- 1 John 1:7 - "we have fellowship with one another"

1. How does the Bible use the term "fellowship?" _____
_____

KITCHENS, FELLOWSHIP HALLS, AND RECREATION

2. Do any of these passages use the term "fellowship" to refer to joint participation in social activities? _____ verse(s) _____

3. Thought question: If we use the term "fellowship" as the Bible does, what is our "fellowship hall?" _____
_____

Appealing to the Sinner

Some churches justify their social activities by saying they are a means to attract people to Christ.

4. What is God's power to save (Rom. 1:16)? _____
_____

5. After Jesus performed the miracle of feeding the 5,000 to prove He was the Messiah, the people followed Him across the Sea of Galilee. What did Jesus say about their motivation to follow Him (John 6:26-27)? _____
_____

   A. Did Jesus continue to feed them with physical bread (John 6:35)? _____
   _____

   B. Jesus said that He was the "Bread of Life". How do we eat this "Bread" (John 6:63)? _____
   _____

   C. What effect did this have on the "disciples" of Christ (John 6:66)? _____
   _____

   D. Peter spoke for those who did not leave Jesus. Why did they not leave (John 6:67-69)? _____
   _____

6. Is there any Biblical authority to attract someone to Christ through social activities? _____ verse(s) _____

Lesson 10

KITCHENS, FELLOWSHIP HALLS, AND RECREATION (2)

The Nature of the Work of the Church

1. What type of kingdom did Jesus establish (John 18:36)? _____
   _____

2. What is the focus of Christ's kingdom (Rom. 14:17)? _____
   _____

3. What is the main responsibility of the church (1 Tim. 3:14-15)? _____
   _____

   A. Scan through the book of 1 Timothy. As Paul told Timothy how he was to conduct himself in the house of God, did he talk about social or spiritual work? _____
   _____
   _____

4. For what were the Thessalonians known (1 Thess. 1:6-10)? _____
   _____

5. When the church was first established, what characterized them (Acts 2:42)? _____
   _____

   A. Who did the church help financially (Acts 2:44-45)? _____
   _____

   B. Did Christians eat together (Acts 2:46)? _____ Where? _____
   _____

6. When Paul tried to correct an abuse of the Lord's supper, what did he say about Christians eating a meal together (1 Cor. 11:22)? _____
   _____

INSTITUTIONALISM

The Work of the Church

7. What does the church have authority to do?

   A. Worship together—Heb. 10:25; Acts 20:7.

   - Can a church build and maintain a building in which to assemble? _____
   _____

   B. Partake of the Lord's supper—1 Cor. 11:20-34.

   - Can a church purchase and maintain trays, a table and other items necessary to partake of the Lord's supper?_____

   C. Give into a common treasury—1 Cor. 16:1-4.

   - Can a church buy baskets or other means to gather and/or store the collection?
   _____

   D. Sing together—1 Cor. 14:23 ; Eph. 5:19.

   - Can a church buy song books or projector to project the songs on a screen? ___
   _____

   E. Pray together—Acts 2:42.

   - Can a church buy a PA system so everyone can hear the prayer? _____
   _____

   F. Teach/preach—Acts 2:42; 20:7.

   - Can a church buy a pulpit and/or rent or build class rooms to assist in the teaching/preaching? _____

   G. Social activities—verse(s) _____

   - Can a church build and maintain a building for the church to meet for social gatherings? _____ verse(s) _____

   - Can a church build and maintain work out facilities like a gym, weight room, room for aerobics, etc.? _____verse(s) _____

   - Can a church hire a man to coordinate social activities? _____ verse(s) __
   _____

DENOMINATIONALISM

Lesson 11

Jesus established one true church and has left detailed instructions for how it is to function. These instructions include everything needed to reproduce the church Jesus built—in any generation, any culture, until this world ends. Denominations, on the other hand, are the product of man. Each denomination is characterized by (1) a unique name, (2) a unique set of beliefs (creed) in addition to the Bible and (3) its own organizational structures. Unfortunately, all three of these qualities are different from and therefore in opposition to Jesus' instructions.

It is the responsibility of every Christian to be part of a local church which is following the pattern of the Head of the church, Jesus.

In the 1800's, a major movement can be traced of men and women who threw off the traditions of man-made religion and went back to the simple pattern of the truth of Jesus. Tremendous growth took place and amazing unity was enjoyed by churches across the country and the world as each followed the teaching of the Lord. Unfortunately, two major divisions have torn the body of Christ asunder. The first occurred around 1900 with the controversy over instrumental music, the missionary society and other innovations. The second occurred in the 1950s and 1960s over institutionalism. In each of these divisions, the more liberal side has progressed toward denominationalism.

In his booklet, *Emergence of the "Church of Christ" Denomination*, Ed Harrell documents the progression toward denominationalism from a historical and sociological viewpoint. Brother Harrell writes:

> The classic pattern involved in a religious division is known as the 'sect of denomination' process. As briefly stated by Ernst Troeltsch, an eminent German historian, all new and fervent religious groups emerge as 'sects.' Troeltsch called the church of the first century a 'sect.' 'Sects,' according to Troeltsch and hundreds of others who have built on this work, have certain definable traits. Their members believe they have 'the truth,' they are strict morally, they believe themselves to be

'the church,' they are fervent, and exhibit other similar characteristics. While one is under no obligation to accept the name 'sect,' there is no question that my religious convictions belong in the conservative realm that sociologists describe with this term. I am not a member of a 'sect,' I'm a Christian and a member of 'the church.' But it is precisely this attitude which, to the modern scholar, means 'sectarianism.'

'Denomination' is the term used by sociologists to describe the other classic religious form in the United States. 'Denominations' have a variety of distinguishable characteristics. They are tolerant of other 'churches,' they generally accept the moral standards of the society in which they exist, they are less dogmatic, less active, and more interested in the world around them.

Sociologists have long recognized that 'sects' tend to evolve into 'denominations.' Countless groups which had their origins as conservative and exclusive churches have evolved in the course of a few generations into liberal and tolerant denominations. Of course, there is usually a small element in any division which clings to the old conservative convictions, refuses to make the transition to liberalism, and usually is forced to separate itself...

The 'sect-to-denomination' process, which is so recurrent in American religious history, is an easily explained phenomenon once these facts are understood. A religious group that begins as the fervent offspring of poor but honest people can change quite decisively in a few generations time. The successful grandchildren and great-grandchildren who have far exceeded their forebearers financially, educationally, and socially are not likely to want the same kind of worship, the same kind of preachers, or the same kind of gospel that their ancestors loved. So they change the church (p.6-8).

This "sect to denomination" progression happened to the Disciples of Christ and is in progress right now in institutional churches of Christ. Since the 1960s, many of these churches have become almost indistinguishable from their denominational friends. Practices which would not have been tolerated a few decades ago are being embraced such as instrumental music, "praise groups," women teaching men, celebrating man-made religious holidays and open fellowship with the denominational world.

The Danger of Denominationalism

1. What are the three characteristics of a denomination?

   A. _____

   B. _____

   C. _____

2. Is denominationalism a work of the flesh or fruit of the Spirit (Gal. 5:19-23)? _____
   _____

3. What is the expressed will of Jesus concerning His followers (John 17:20-21)? ___
   _____

4. What did the children of Israel want and why (1 Sam. 8:5)? _____
   _____

   A. How could that same attitude be expressed in the Lord's church today? _____
   _____

   B. Why is this such a powerful temptation? _____
   _____

5. What problem existed in the church at Corinth (1 Cor. 1:10-13)? _____
   _____

   A. What was the solution (1 Cor. 1:18; 2:1-5; 4:6)? _____
   _____

6. What is to be our mentality toward those in denominations (Luke 19:10; Matt. 28:18-20)? _____
   _____

   - 2 Cor. 6:14-18 - _____
   _____

   - 1 John 4:1 - _____
   _____

   - 2 John 9-11 - _____
   _____

7. Are all saved people in the church of Christ (Acts 2:38-41,47; Eph. 1:22-23)? _____
   _____

DENOMINATIONALISM (2)

Lesson 12

An illustration of the progression toward denominationalism in many institutional churches of Christ is the Herald of Truth. Bill Hall, in his lesson on the sponsoring church arrangement said, "a major change took place in the preaching on the Herald of Truth. He [citing Richard Hughes, professor at Pepperdine University and writer of Reviving the Ancient Faith] says that when the Herald of Truth first began, the preaching was focused on the one true church, baptism for the remission of sins, no instrumental music, the Lord's Supper every first day of the week. It was convincing people regarding the idea of restoring New Testament Christianity. But by the late '60s and early '70s, they had begun to realize that the radio and TV programs that were really attracting the audiences were those that's emphasis was more on family relationships, finding inner peace for yourself, how to build a strong self-image. Eventually the preaching of the Herald of Truth shifted from this more doctrinal, controversial type of teaching into this more 'finding peace for the soul and a good self-image' type of teaching. Now, he said, all the preachers made the same shift, so that by the '70s and '80s you could attend most churches of Christ for months and months and months and months and never hear a sermon on the one true church, restoring New Testament Christianity, or instrumental music."

Name

1. What are some of the terms used to describe individual followers of Christ?

    A. Acts 11:26 - _____

    B. Acts 11:29 - _____

    C. 1 Cor. 1:2 - _____

    D. 1 Pet. 2:5 - _____

2. By whose name are we saved (Acts 4:12)? _____
_____

A. Is there one particular name that we should wear? _____ verse(s) _____
_____

B. Can we name ourselves after a particular man or religious belief? _____
verse(s) _____

C. Are churchachrister or CoC proper designations for followers of Christ? _____
verse(s) _____

3. What are some of the terms used to describe the local group of Christians?

A. Rom. 16:16 - _____

B. I Cor. 1:2 - _____

C. 1 Cor. 3:16 - _____

D. Eph. 2:19 - _____

E. Col. 1:13 - _____

F. Is there one particular name the local church should wear? _____
verse(s) _____

G. Are there any "churchachrist preachers" found in the Bible? _____
verse(s) _____

4. What indicates when a name has become denominational rather than Biblical? __
_____
_____

Creed

5. What are we to believe and teach (Matt. 28:18-20; 2 Tim. 1:13; Jude 3)? _____
_____

6. Do we need anything more than the Bible as our guide (2 Tim. 3:16-17; 2 Pet. 1:3)?
_____

7. Whose approval do we seek above all (2 Tim. 2:14-18)? _____
_____

DENOMINATIONALISM (2)

A. Are we to teach "churchachrist doctrine"? _____ verse(s) _____
_____

B. When in a religious conversation, should our emphasis be on what our church teaches? _____ If not, what should it be on? _____

C. Should we only hire "churchachrist preachers"? _____ verse(s) _____
_____

8. What indicates when teaching has become denominational rather than Biblical?
_____
_____

Organization

9. Since we have studied extensively the Lord's pattern for the organization of the local church in previous lessons, please summarize the Lord's pattern. _____
_____

10. What indicates when organization has become denominational rather than Biblical? _____
_____

www.ingramcontent.com/pod-product-compliance
Lightning Source LLC
Chambersburg PA
CBHW081354040426
42450CB00016B/3440